Easy Grammar Grade 6

Student Test Booklet

Wanda C. Phillips

Easy Grammar Systems

SCOTTSDALE, ARIZONA 85255

© 2006

TABLE OF CONTENTS

TESTS

Name_____   **PRE-ASSESSMENT**

Date_____

A. Sentence Types:
        Directions: Place correct punctuation at the end of each sentence
                   and write the sentence type on the line.

1. _____   Does he have a fever

2. _____   Mark eats at his office desk

3. _____   Stand at this line

4. _____   I'm so excited

B. Sentences, Fragments, and Run-Ons:
        Directions: Write **S** if the words form a sentence. Write **F** if the words
                   form a fragment. Write **R-O** if the words form a run-on.

1. ____   Watch out!

2. ____   After they play tennis.

3. ____   On the evening before departing on a cruise to the island of Aruba.

4. ____   You seem cold, here take my extra blanket.

5. ____   We have a new postal lady.

C. Friendly Letters:
        Directions: Label the parts of this friendly letter:

                                                             2 Sea Way
                    _____   **Otter Rock, OR   97388**
                                                   August 2, 20—

Dear Lani,   _____

        Hi! I just want to give you our new address. We moved to Otter Rock
a few months ago. Oregon is so green from rain. It's a great place to hike, too!
Did you know that it is light until about nine here in the summer? _____

                                        Love, _____
                                        Amy _____

D. Business Letters:
    Directions: Label the boldfaced part of this business letter *and* punctuate the salutation (greeting) correctly.

September 21, 20—

Success Concepts
Post Office Box 12
Scottsdale, AZ   85155
                   _____

Dear Mr. Phipps

E. Envelopes:
    Directions: Write your return address on this envelope. (You may create an address if you wish.)
_____

   _____

   _____

   _____

                     _____

                     _____

                     _____

_____

F. Capitalization:
    Directions: Write a capital letter above any word that should be capitalized.

1. did general washington lead the continental army during the revolutionary war?

2. students from price middle school visited a spanish church in alamo square.

3. Last sunday, she entered davis memorial hospital for diabetes testing.

4. has dad learned about the roman empire in his college world history class?

5. can i take a ferry from ratton bay to ocracoke lighthouse in the south next fall?

6. mary pickford starred in an early movie entitled <u>tess of the storm country</u>.

2

G. Punctuation:
   Directions: Insert needed punctuation.

1. Tate asked Wheres Peters black two piece suit

2. Judd meet me at 4 30 by the town hall the brick building on N Rue Way

3. On Friday May 20 2005 their son flew home and they all went out to celebrate

4. No we arent leaving for Sweet Grass Montana until our two sons game is over.

5. Ms Luna by the way has donated the following items beads sequins and wire

6. Yippee exclaimed Maria You won a prize a gift certificate for twenty dollars

H. Subjects and Verbs:
   Directions: Underline the subject once and the verb or verb phrase twice.
   Note: Crossing out prepositional phrases will help you.

1. Before bedtime, the young father likes to sit by his daughter's cradle.

2. Someone like Mark should apply for that job.

3. Joe and his son cannot lift this into the truck without your help.

4. Each of the students in that class must present a speech.

5. Follow the sidewalk by the well-lighted alley.

I. Contractions:
   Directions: Write the contraction.

1. cannot - _____   3. you are - _____   5. will not - _____

2. what is - _____   4. they have - _____   6. they are - _____

J. Subject-Verb Agreement:
   Directions: Underline the subject once. Underline the verb that agrees twice.

1. Their parents (belong, belongs) to a fishing club.

2. This splinter on my right thumb (hurt, hurts).

3. Only one of the new flight attendants (is, are) twenty-one.   3

K.   Irregular Verbs:
   Directions: Underline the subject once and the correct verb phrase twice.

1.   Their windshield has been (broke, broken).

2.   By the end of the day, we will have (run, ran) two miles.

3.   Pets were (brung, brought) along.

4.   I must have (done, did) the wrong assignment.

5.   Have you (saw, seen) a yak?

6.   The seeds may have (sank, sunk) to the bottom of the pot.

7.   Wind must have (blown, blew) that tree down.

8.   I could not have (chose, chosen) a better gift.

9.   One of the swimmers has (swam, swum) in three races.

10.   The newspaper is (lying, laying) on a table.

11.   Sara might have (wrote, written) us a note.

12.   Jess had (drunk, drank) some orange juice.

13.   Some may have (went, gone) ahead.

14.   The children have (come, came) late for the performance.

15.   They should have (raised, risen) earlier.

L.   Tenses:
   Directions: Underline the subject once and the verb or verb phrase
                        twice.   Write the tense in the blank.

1.   _____   Will you join our team?

2.   _____   Leah peered through the telescope.

3.   _____   Cole weaves rugs.

4

M. Common and Proper Nouns:
   Directions: Place a ✓ if the noun is abstract.

1. _____ care   2. _____ carton   3. _____ patience

N. Singular and Plural Nouns:
   Directions: Write the correct spelling of each plural noun.

1. guess - _____   5. journey - _____

2. waltz - _____   6. paradox - _____

3. chairwoman - _____   7. courage - _____

4. penalty - _____   8. serf - _____

O. Possessive Nouns:
   Directions: Write the possessive in each blank.

1. an office building owned by more than one businessman -

   _____

2. a play area used by monkeys - _____

3. a trunk belonging to an elephant - _____

4. a vehicle belonging to Debi and Judi - _____

P. Identifying Nouns:
   Directions: Circle any nouns.

1. My idea is to take this shovel, a sleeping bag, two tents, and some strong rope.

Q. Usage and Knowledge:

1. Circle the correct answer: Do you know if (there, they're, their) in
                                kindergarten?

2. Circle the correct answer: (Can, May) I come in?   5

3. Circle the correct answer: They completed the job (themselves, theirselves).

4. Write the antecedent of the possessive pronoun. Many eagles flew to their nests. _____

5. Place a dotted line under an interjection and a wavy line under a conjunction.

   Stand still or you may fall! Yikes!

6. Write a regular verb: _____

7. Circle the correct answer: You did that (perfect, perfectly).

8. Write a proper noun: _____

9. Circle the correct answer: I didn't buy (any, none).

10. Circle the correct answer: Our team played (good, well).

11. Write the antecedent of the possessive pronoun:

    You must give your full name. _____

12. Write a reflexive pronoun: _____

R. Identifying Adjectives:
   Directions: Circle any adjective.

1. An artist painted several bright blue flowers on two Chinese brass vases.

S. Degrees of Adjectives:
   Directions: Circle the correct answer.

1. This is the (more beautiful, most beautiful) ring of the entire collection.

2. This red helium balloon is (shinier, shiniest) of the five.

3. The taller of the two wrestlers is (more powerful, most powerful).

4. He is the (more respectful, most respectful) twin.

T. Adverbs:
     Directions: Circle any adverbs.

1. Jacy looks pale and doesn't feel very (good, well).

2. Stop acting so (weird, weirdly).

3. We don't want (none, any).

U. Identifying Adverbs:
     Directions: Circle any adverbs.

1. Two rather large dogs ran wildly together.

2. We will not arrive there tomorrow.

V. Degrees of Adverbs:
     Directions: Circle the correct answer.

1. Jack did his fourth exercise (more strenously, most strenuously).

2. Of the two contestants, Chessa throws the ball (harder, hardest).

3. That baby slept (more peacefully, most peacefully) on the third night.

4. I did (worse, worser, worst, worsest) on my second try.

W. Pronouns:
     Directions: Circle the correct answer.

1. Ringo, Hans, and (he, him) bought tickets for a ride.

2. (Me and my brother, My brother and me, My brother and I) are sweaty.

3. The ushers are Jana and (I, me).

4. I like (them, those) sparkling wands.

5. After the game, meet my brother and (I, me) outside.

6. Kim and (we, us) must finish putting away these tools.

7. (Who, Whom) did you ask?

8. Did the gardener and (they, them) seed the lawn?

9. The first ones chosen were Kate and (he, him).

10. My hair has lost (its, it's) luster.

11. Margo's brothers lost (his, their) place in line.

12. The boss handed Ben and (she, her) several packages.

13. (Who, Whom) is the artist of this modern painting?

14. Each of the women handed (her, their) keys to the valet.

15. One of the horses ran toward (its, their) colts.

X. Nouns and Pronouns Used as Subjects, Direct Objects, Indirect Objects, Objects of the Preposition, and Predicate Nominatives:

Directions: Look at the boldfaced word and decide how it is used in the sentence. Write **S.** for subject, **D.O.** for direct object, **I.O.** for indirect object, **O.P.** for object of the preposition, and **P.N.** for predicate nominative.

1. ____ Their **boss** quit yesterday.

2. ____ Terry is our **leader**.

3. ____ The dentist cleaned my **teeth**.

4. ____ She has gum in her **hair**.

5. ____ Mary and **I** play together.

8

Date_____

Directions: Cross out any prepositional phrase(s). Underline the subject once and the verb/verb phrase twice. Starred sentences contain helping verb(s).

1. I went to a store at the mall.

2. Some islands are off the coast of California.

3. A picture is on the wall above a computer.

4. Mark and his cousin walked down the street toward the loggers.

5. After lunch, some of the boys play ping pong.

6. A swimmer dashed out the door and jumped into the water.

7. Throughout the day, many roofers rested under a huge willow tree.

8. A letter from Cindy and Sandy arrived in the mail today.

9. During the festival, people went into the hall to eat.

10. An airplane rolled down the runway without lights.

11. Before the storm, our dog came inside for shelter.

12. *Their friend has been without electricity since the tornado.

13. *A decision regarding freeways will not be made until February.

14. Put this bag of trash by the front door.

15. *The red tile was replaced with white tile and carpeting.

Name_____   **VERB TEST**

Date_____

A. Directions: Write the contraction.

1. had not - _____   6. where is - _____

2. I have - _____   7. will not - _____

3. we will - _____   8. what is - _____

4. do not - _____   9. I am - _____

5. they are - _____   10. he is - _____

B. Directions: Cross out any prepositional phrase(s). Underline the subject once
    and the verb/verb phrase twice.

1. A sunbather has (went, gone) into the water.

2. The mail had (come, came) earlier in the day.

3. One of the sheep has (lain, laid) in the field.

4. Aaron must have (drank, drunk) a quart of juice.

5. Our team should have (taken, took) the lead from the opponents

6. Clara may have (brang, brought) her brother to the party.

7. An envelope without a stamp has (fallen, fell) on the ground.

8. Have you (rode, ridden) your bike?

9. I could have (ate, eaten) more hot dogs for lunch.

10. One of the swimmers must have (drove, driven) to the shore.

C. Directions: Cross out any prepositional phrase(s). Underline the subject once and the verb/verb phrase twice. Write the tense: *present*, *past*, or *future* in the space provided.

1. _____ I shall demand an answer from him.

2. _____ A lizard crawls up our wall.

3. _____ A group of teenagers ate taffy at the fair.

4. _____ The children build castles in the sand.

5. _____ We will attend the wedding during the evening.

6. _____ Lemons are in the refrigerator.

7. _____ Matthew read the map with a flashlight.

8. _____ Linda and Danny work at a factory.

9. _____ A musician played a song about love.

10. _____ His dad will remain in the service until his retirement.

D. Directions: Cross out any prepositional phrase(s). Underline the subject once and the verb twice.

1. A snail (moves, move) slowly.

2. Several ducks (waddle, waddles) around that park.

3. Mom and Dad (shops, shop) for our groceries.

4. These apples (tastes, taste) sour.

5. Jackie (spend, spends) so much time on her hair.

6. Todd and I (is, are) in the band.

7. That child (sings, sing) to her little brother.

8. Those lifeguards (save, saves) the lives of many people.

9. Everyone of the boys (are, is) in my Sunday school class.

10. That family and she (ski, skis) at a winter camp.

E. Directions: Cross out any prepositional phrase(s). Underline the subject once and the verb twice. Write A if the verb is action and L if the verb is linking.

1. _____   Her hairbrush remained dirty.

2. _____   A girl with long hair stayed excited for a long time.

3. _____   Several chefs tasted the winning veal dinner.

4. _____   The chimes at the tower sound pretty.

5. _____   Her short story became funny.

F. Directions: Cross out any prepositional phrase(s). Underline the subject once and the verb/verb phrase twice.

1. A hamster is sitting on our sidewalk.

2. Many large hotels have been built in Scottsdale.

3. A robber and his girlfriend fled from the bank.

4. Take this to the train station with you.

5. Are the tourists visiting those old castles?

6. Two businessmen met and ate lunch at the Kettle Inn.

7. You will not be given another dish of chocolate pudding.

8. May we mow your grass with this electric lawn mower?

9. Each of the parents had been sent a note concerning flu shots.

10. Would you please hand this ticket to the bus driver?

Name_____   **NOUN TEST**

Date_____

A. Directions: Write <u>A</u> if the noun is abstract; write <u>C</u> if the noun is concrete.

1. _____   grace   6. _____   happiness

2. _____   ladder   7. _____   window

3. _____   marshmallow   8. _____   air

4. _____   safety   9. _____   pamphlet

5. _____   bulb   10. _____   patience

B. Directions: Write <u>C</u> if the noun is common; write <u>P</u> if the noun is proper.

1. _____   LONDON BRIDGE   6. _____   MUSEUM

2. _____   SOUP   7. _____   PLUM

3. _____   SNAKE   8. _____   SENATOR JONES

4. _____   COPPERHEAD SNAKE   9. _____   FRUIT

5. _____   PHOENIX ART MUSEUM 10. _____   MEXICO

C. Directions: Write <u>A</u> if the underlined word serves as an adjective (describing
                word); write <u>N</u> if the word serves as a noun.

1. _____   The dog chewed a <u>bone</u>.

2. _____   This catalog offers <u>bone</u> china.

3. _____   The <u>cave</u> explorer has arrived.

4. _____   Would you like to visit a <u>cave</u> in Kentucky?

D. Directions: Write <u>V</u> if the underlined word serves as a verb; write <u>N</u> if the underlined word serves as a noun.

1. _____   The girls <u>laugh</u> together often.

2. _____   My <u>laugh</u> is soft but funny.

3. _____   They made a <u>paste</u> from flour and water.

4. _____   <u>Paste</u> this magazine picture on the white paper.

E. Directions: Write the possessive form.

1. a chicken belonging to Susie: _____

2. books belonging to that boy: _____

3. parents belonging to Chris: _____

4. a playground belonging to children: _____

5. a horse path for riders: _____

6. a master of more than one ox: _____

F. Directions: Write the plural form:

1. dash - _____   6. box - _____

2. fly - _____   7. toy - _____

3. sock - _____   8. table - _____

4. leaf - _____   9. pass - _____

5. bench - _____   10. sheep - _____

16

G. Directions: Write the determiner and the noun in the space provided.

1. Some wild geese flew overhead.   _____

2. He ate three bread sticks.   _____

3. Give me your money, please.   _____

4. They didn't like the movie.   _____

5. Arnie's uncle left today.   _____

H. Directions: Box any noun.

1. The volunteers picked up some garbage in the alley.

2. The man had thirteen stitches in his right leg.

3. Several actors perform on a stage without a microphone.

4. An elephant walked through the jungle during a rainstorm.

5. Jimmy's roller blades and his bike are on a pile beside the garage.

6. Their aunt made apple pies, a cake, and punch for the party.

7. Carla showed her concern for the child with a gentle hug.

8. Grandma showed pictures of her friends' homes in Denver.

9. Many bugs were crawling in our flowers by those sheds.

10. Your love for the outdoors was shown during that camping trip.

Name_____   **CUMULATIVE TEST**
                                              Nouns
Date_____

A.   Directions: Cross out any prepositional phrase(s).   Underline the subject once
                   and the verb twice.

1. Two children dashed up the hill in a race.

2. Everyone except the mother of the bride was ready.

3. Underneath the palm tree sat a beachcomber.

4. The car backed out of the driveway very slowly.

5. One of the puppets has brown hair with red bows.

6. The band director and music teacher sing in our church choir.

7. Take this bag of popcorn to the baseball game tonight.

B.   Directions: Cross out any prepositional phrase(s). Underline the subject once
                   and the verb/verb phrase twice. Label any direct object -D.O.

1. A burglar in a white car had (stole, stolen) a television.

2. One of the bags has (broke, broken) at the bottom.

3. Mrs. Jansen had (laid, lay) the dress in the box.

4. The pilot must have (flown, flew) to Turkey.

5. My brother might have (ate, eaten) the roast beef sandwich.

6. Darla's mother has (risen, rose) to a supervisor in the company.

C.   Directions: Cross out any prepositional phrase(s). Underline the subject once
                   and the verb/verb phrase twice. Write the tense, *present*, *past*, or
                   future, in the space provided.

1. _____   His sister teaches their dog tricks.

2. _____   Mr. Jacobson fell into the pool recently.

3. _____   The soccer players will practice before the game.

4. _____   Two wrestlers are in the state championship.

5. _____   Some shrubs and flowers grow better in the shade.

19

Name_____   **ADJECTIVE TEST**

Date_____

A. Directions: Circle any proper adjective and capitalize it. In the space provided,
                 write the proper adjective and the noun it modifies.

1. Winter snows block some arizona highways.   _____

2. A japanese bonsai tree is pretty.   _____

3. Did they take a taxi to the denver hotel?   _____

4. The tourists admired the english countryside.   _____

5. Come to my house for a christmas feast.   _____

6. Pedro rides a schwinn bicycle.   _____

B. Directions: Cross out any prepositional phrase(s). Underline the subject once
                 and the verb/verb phrase twice. Label any predicate adjective-P.A.
                 Write the predicate adjective and the noun it modifies on the line.

                                               P.A.
         Example: The mud <u>flaps</u> ~~on this car~~ <u>are</u> too low.   <u>low flaps</u>_____

1. His voice suddenly sounded squeaky.   _____   _____

2. The battery in the yellow car is dead.   _____

3. Her knee becomes painful during rain.   _____

4. Those towels are damp from baths.   _____

5. The apple cobbler smells good.   _____

21

C. Directions: Circle any adjectives.

Remember: **First, circle any limiting adjective(s). Next, reread the sentence and circle any descriptive adjective(s).**

1. Venus is a brilliant planet in our solar system.

2. His final payment on the ruby ring was twenty dollars.

3. A few toads hopped along the dusty country lane.

4. Erin's first Easter basket was shaped like a gigantic egg.

5. They wore wet suits in the icy waters on that foggy day.

6. These large greeting cards with the funny kittens are cute.

7. An orange tricycle was given to the surprised child on his fourth birthday.

8. Several paper towels were scattered on the dirty floor of the boys' bathroom.

D. Directions: Circle the correct adjective form.

1. Jeremiah is the (smaller, smallest) twin.

2. Jim Thorpe was one of the (faster, fastest) runners in the world.

3. Roy is (cheerfuler, more cheerful) than his older brother.

4. She is the (more pleasant, most pleasant) prom queen ever.

5. The first swimmer has a (better, best) stroke than his opponent.

6. Of the three tires, this one is (more damaged, most damaged.)

7. My mother is (more patient, most patient) with me than my sister.

8. This is the (more beautiful, most beautiful) spot in the world.

22

Name_____   **CUMULATIVE TEST**
                                                      Adjectives

Date_____

A.   Directions: Cross out any prepositional phrase(s).   Underline the subject once
                    and the verb/verb phrase twice. Label any direct object-<u>D.O.</u>

1.   The hot air balloon with red stripes left before dawn.

2.   The argument between the two men was about higher taxes.

3.   Some of the boys picked berries along the country road.

4.   Beneath the bridge the woman sat during hot summer days.

5.   All the children but Lenny found Easter eggs among the various plants.

B.   Directions: Cross out any prepositional phrase(s).   Underline the subject once
                    and the verb/verb phrase twice.

   1.   Only one man (travel, travels) alone.

   2.   His truck has (fell, fallen) into a ditch.

   3.   Has Jim (took, taken) a tent on his camping trip?

   4.   The sun has already (risen, rose).

   5.   A large pink balloon without any ribbon has (burst, busted).

   6.   Those bowlers (score, scores) strikes often.

   7.   Does Jane (sit, set) in the middle of the front row?

   8.   One of the hotel guests (eat, eats) meals by the pool.

   9.   Kirby (lay, laid) an apple under some papers near the sink.

   10.   Mr. Greer (rose, raised) until the end of the national anthem.

   11.   An alligator had (swam, swum) past the small boat in the Everglades.

   12.   Should you have (knew, known) the man across the street?

   13.   Many people (go, goes) through that mountain tunnel.

   14.   The lady was (swore, sworn) in during the trial.

   15.   This package has been (lying, laying) here all afternoon.   23

C. Directions: Write the contraction on the line.

1. I have - _____ 3. you are - _____ 5. cannot - _____

2. was not - _____ 4. who is - _____ 6. we will - _____

D. Directions: Cross out any prepositional phrase(s). Underline the subject once and the verb/verb phrase twice. Write the tense: *present, past,* or *future* on the line.

1. _____ Paul will send this for you.

2. _____ A mason laid bricks during the afternoon.

3. _____ Those tree limbs are by the dumpster.

4. _____ My friend's dad walks several miles before breakfast.

E. Directions: Fill in the blank:

1. Write an interjection: _____

2. The three coordinating conjunctions are _____, _____, and _____.

3. Write an abstract noun: _____

4. Write a proper noun: _____

5. *He had not gone.:* verb phrase:_____, main verb:_____

F. Directions: Write the plural.

1. cemetery - _____ 4. half - _____

2. prayer - _____ 5. tomato - _____

3. monkey - _____ 6. mouse - _____

G. Directions: Write the possessive form.

1. turtles belonging to a girl - _____

2. whiffle ball belonging to two boys - _____

3. meeting belonging to more than one woman - _____

24

H. Directions: Box any noun.

Remember: **Determining (limiting) adjectives often help you find nouns.**

1. Two baby teeth are sticking out of his swollen gums.

2. Mo's mother lives in Texas with twelve cats and an oversized dog.

3. A letter from Mrs. Kelly arrived by special delivery in the afternoon.

4. Many little monkeys were swinging from large bars.

5. Her response was a happy scream and a hug for all her friends.

6. I camped beside a lake in the mountains of Missouri.

I. Directions: Fill in the blank.

1. *Put this envelope on the desk.* The subject of this sentence is _____.

2. Write the past participle form of the following verbs:

   A. to come - (had) _____   D. to walk - (had) _____

   B. to live - (had) _____   E. to sink - (had) _____

   C. to teach - (had) _____   F. to give - (had) _____

Free A: (one additional point for each correct answer)

1. Not is never a _____.

2. The word that ends a prepositional phrase is called the _____ of the preposition. Example: down the **street**

3. A regular verb adds _____ at the end in both the past tense and the past participle form. Write an example of a regular verb: _____

4. To + verb is called an _____.

5. *Mr. Hamilton handed Molly a check.* The indirect object of this sentence is

   _____.

25

Name_____   **ADVERB TEST**

Date_____

A.   Directions: Circle any adverb(s).

1.   You must sign here carefully, but write quickly.

2.   Tonight they will be taking a rather short walk up into the mountains.

3.   He always writes neatly, but he drops his papers everywhere.

4.   Sal arises early and fishes upstream daily.

5.   Harvey hit the ball very hard out into left field.

6.   The attendant clearly announced that the flight would not arrive late.

B.   Directions: Choose the correct adverb.

1.   That announcer speaks (more rapidly, most rapidly) than his friend.

2.   Jill runs (faster, faster) than her sister.

3.   Of the four, this large balloon rose (more quickly, most quickly).

4.   Mark walks (more slowly, most slowly) than I.

5.   Chelsea arrived (earlier, earliest) of all the students.

6.   Of all the diagrams, this one was drawn (more carefully, most carefully).

C.   Directions: Select the correct word.

1.   Mrs. Reno doesn't eat (any, no) chicken.

2.   That girl swims so (good, well).

3.   He never has (no, any) money.

4.   Nobody wants (anything, nothing) from the snack bar.

5.   Their sister hasn't felt (good, well) all week.   27

Date_____

A. Directions: Select the correct pronoun.

 1.   The missionary spoke to (them, they) about Peru.

 2.   (I, Me) like to read about lizards.

 3.   The babysitter read (we, us) a story about whales.

 4.   The second speaker is (she, her).

 5.   (Who, Whom) has the time?

 6.   A lifeguard teaches (they, them) swimming strokes.

 7.   With (who, whom) has she planned the picnic?

 8.   The disagreement was between Teresa and (she, her).

 9.   Are (we, us) boys invited?

10.   Ask (we, us) friends to help you.

B. Directions: Write P in the blank if the underlined word serves as a pronoun; write
                         A in the blank if the underlined word serves as an adjective.

1. _____   Can you imagine that?

2. _____   This video machine is broken.

3. _____   Which car is longer?

4. _____   Have you decided whose shoes are in the laundry room?

5. _____   What do you want?

C. Directions: Select the correct word.

1. Are you aware that (it's, its) raining?

2. She doesn't know (their, they're) address.

3. Joe makes (his, their) own bed.

4. The giraffe moved (it's, its) neck slowly.

5. Some basketball players help (his, their) communities by raising money for charity.

6. Both want (his, their) dinner on a paper plate.

7. Everyone of the students took (his, their) books.

8. Janice and (we, us) talked about our camping trip.

9. The winners of the art contest were Darlene and (him, he).

10. The child couldn't reach the cookie jar (hisself, himself).

D. Directions: Write the antecedent of the underlined word.

1. _____ That book has lost its cover.

2. _____ Do most hikers take their canteens everywhere?

3. _____ Charles and I eat our dinner early.

4. _____ You must take your own money.

5. _____ Each of the spaniels ran to his owner.

E. Directions: Tell how the underlined pronoun functions in the sentence.
    A. subject   B. direct object   C. Indirect object
    D. object of the preposition   E. predicate nominative

1. _____ Your aunt helped me.

2. _____ May I go with them?

3. _____ A senator gave us a tour of the senate building.

4. _____ He is playing with his cousin.

5. _____ The last person in line was she.
30

A.   Directions: List 50 prepositions.

1. _____   14. _____   27. _____   40. _____

2. _____   15. _____   28. _____   41. _____

3. _____   16. _____   29. _____   42. _____

4. _____   17. _____   30. _____   43. _____

5. _____   18. _____   31. _____   44. _____

6. _____   19. _____   32. _____   45. _____

7. _____   20. _____   33. _____   46. _____

8. _____   21. _____   34. _____   47. _____

9. _____   22. _____   35. _____   48. _____

10. _____   23. _____   36. _____   49. _____

11. _____   24. _____   37. _____   50. _____

12. _____   25. _____   38. _____

13. _____   26. _____   39. _____

B.   Directions: Cross out any prepositional phrase(s).   Underline the subject once
     and the verb/verb phrase twice.   Label any direct object-<u>D.O.</u>

1.   The screen on the back window has several holes.

2.   The man in the white shirt eats a sandwich at a deli every day.

3.   One lady without an umbrella dashed out into the rain.

4.   Your fan above the coffee table has unusual blades.

5.   Everyone but Claire sat beneath the tree and talked.

C. Directions: Cross out any prepositional phrase(s). Underline the subject once and the verb/verb phrase twice.

1. That man (go, goes) to his office in the evening, too.

2. Has your balloon (busted, burst)?

3. Her arm was (broke, broken) during the fall.

4. Several companies (washes, wash) windows in tall buildings.

5. Did you (sit, set) the alarm?

6. His little boat had (sank, sunk) in the puddle.

7. Several people (walk, walks) through the park each evening.

8. You could not have (chosen, chose) a better one.

9. Have you (drank, drunk) milk for lunch?

10. The newspaper is (laying, lying) on the floor.

11. Missy has (given, gave) her brother some popcorn.

12. Where have you (laid, lain) the clipper?

13. The sun has already (raised, risen).

14. The mail may have (came, come) early.

15. I should have (went, gone) alone.

16. Joan always (sits, sets) in the back row.

17. He could not have (knew, known) that!

18. His answer may have been (wrote, written) on the last page.

19. She must have (rode, ridden) her sister's scooter without permission.

20. One of the boys (flies, fly) kites frequently.

32

D. Directions: Write the contraction.

1. I will - _____ 3. has not - _____ 5. did not - _____

2. who is - _____ 4. we have - _____ 6. I am - _____

E. Directions: Write the sentence type: declarative (statement), imperative (command), interrogative (question), or exclamatory.

1. _____ When does the bus arrive?

2. _____ Drats! I've lost it again!

3. _____ Throw this in the garbage.

4. _____ A bottle was given to the baby.

F. Direction: Write the tense: present, past, or future.

Suggestion: **Cross out any prepositional phrase(s). Underline the subject once and the verb/verb phrase twice.   This will help you determine tense.**

1. _____ I shall give this to your dad.

2. _____ Several chickens in the yard cackled loudly.

3. _____ Rena sleeps late on the weekends.

4. _____ The road near the stop sign is curvy.

G. Directions: Write A if the noun is abstract; write C if the noun is concrete.

1. _____ happiness   3. _____   cucumber

2. _____ quilt   4. _____   peace

H. Directions: Write C if the noun is common; write P if the noun is proper.

1. _____ MR. BARNES 3. _____ OAK   5. _____ CANDLESTICK PARK

2. _____ TREE   4. _____ CITY   6. _____ NEW ORLEANS

I. Directions: Write the plural.

1. solo - _____

2. bush - _____

3. moose - _____

4. spoof - _____

5. baby - _____

6. stitch - _____

7. wrinkle - _____

8. calf - _____

J. Directions: Write the possessive.

1. a uniform belonging to a nurse - _____

2. a bus belonging to tourists - _____

3. a restroom for more than one man - _____

4. a trail that walkers use - _____

K. Directions: Box any nouns.
Remember: Finding determining (limiting) adjectives helps you to find some nouns.

1. Your pizza is in a box in the refrigerator.

2. Several lamps had been purchased for Annie's new home.

3. Nick has two rabbits and many cats in his yard.

4. Some lemons and an orange are needed for that dessert.

5. Are those boys and girls by the lake your relatives?

L. Directions: Read each group of words. Write F̲ for fragment, S̲ for sentence, and
                        R̲-O̲ for run-on.

1. _____   Running down the stairs.

2. _____   We spent the morning doing laundry.

3. _____   His parents went to England, they saw many castles.

4. _____   Left without his baseball mitt or bat.

34

M. Directions: Circle any adjectives.

Suggestion: **Read each sentence and first circle limiting adjectives. Then, reread the sentence and circle descriptive adjectives.**

1. A beautiful flower garden is by that stream.

2. Her older sister and one brother live in an old country inn in Vermont.

3. My German friend attends a private school in a nearby town.

4. Some garlic potatoes and glazed ham were part of the delicious buffet.

5. A talented student wrote a true story about her strange vacation.

N. Directions: Select the correct form.

1. Paulette is (younger, youngest) in her class.

2. Of all our neighbors, Kim is (kinder, kindest).

3. She is the (rowdier, rowdiest) twin.

4. Marlo's office is the (larger, largest) one in the entire building complex.

5. This scarf is (more gorgeous, most gorgeous) than mine.

O. Directions: Circle any adverb.

Suggestion: **Cross out any prepositional phrase(s). Underline the subject once and the verb/verb phrase twice. First, look for any adverbs telling *to what extent*. (They may be in a prepositional phrase, also.) Then, read each sentence looking for any adverbs that tell *how*. Next, look for adverbs that tell *when*. Last, look for adverbs telling *where*.**

1. The boat was rocked very gently by the giggling children.

2. Mr. and Mrs. Fleming go there often.

3. Patiently, the clerks searched in among the clothes racks for the lost child.

4. Those candles did not burn properly.

5. Suddenly, the wind blew quite hard.

Name_____   **CAPITALIZATION TEST**

Date_____

Directions: Write the capital letter above any word that needs to be capitalized.

1.   6228 east bridge street
                                                        arlington, texas   76017
                                                        december 2, 20--

   dear dorothy,

        i'm just letting you know that we will definitely be there for
   christmas vacation.

                                                        truly yours,
                                                        ann

2.   did king david write songs to honor god?

3.   on the last sunday in july they left for a palm springs hotel.

4.   both coach benson and gretta's mom will help with the brightly baseball club.

5.   joanna eats french toast nearly every morning at wren's family restaurant.

6.   next spring the zent family will visit everglades national park in florida.

7.   lenny and uncle fred crossed over the colorado river at the city of yuma.

8.   in reading class, the student read the cat ate my gym suit for a book report.

9.   did general harris and miss bronson meet at the university of hawaii?

10.   his home is located north of mustang library on apple avenue.

11.   the cherry blossom festival is held each year in washington, d. c.

12.   "please sit beside me," said randy.

13.   a christian missionary went to zambia, a country in africa.

14.   did herman fly into los angeles international airport last father's day?

15. for st. valentine's day, mom received jojo's* candy and an italian purse.

16. during the winter, they volunteered at rose garden nursing home.

17. his brother sent dutch tulips as a gift for grandma polley's birthday.

18. i. land vehicles
    a. trucks
    b. vans
    c. cars

    ii. air vehicles
    a. hot air balloons
    b. airplanes

19. in english class, professor gordon taught <u>the tale of two cities</u>.

20. a <u>bible</u> school was held at a lutheran church in bergen county.

21. is ursala's father the leader of the potts valley chamber of commerce?

22. they drive across the oakland bay bridge to their office in san francisco.

23. his neighbor owns barlett bowling alley located in the western part of dell city.

24. mr. a. sabo was admitted to fairwell memorial hospital for kidney stones.

25. the book, <u>my mother doesn't like to cook,</u> was illustrated by micah claycamp.

26. his grandfather is a sheriff for the maricopa county sheriffs' department.

27. kammie and i are going to lake okeechobee and to kitty world.

28. did the american red cross send help to victims of the midwest floods?

29. wilma rode arabian horses on an arizona ranch during her break from penn state university.

30. margot and leonardo yelled, "look at our new prontigo* van!"

*brand name

Name_____   **PUNCTUATION TEST**

Date_____

Directions: Insert any needed punctuation.

    Example: Dear Sir**:**

1. Wow Your ten speed bicycle is great

2. Mr Dave E Loy Capt Fudd and Dad met in Tucson Arizona last fall

3. A large unusual monument will be dedicated at 7 30 P M today

4. Dear Lottie

    I ll go with you to Dannys swim party on Tues August 4

              Your friend
              Bobbie

5. Send the postcard to 24 Briar Lane Napa CA 94558

6. Kirk we need the following clay 3 bottles of paint and glue

7. Kay asked Wheres my lunch sack

8. The one boys grandmother read the nursery rhyme entitled Jack Sprat to him

9. The girls choir cant meet until next Thursday

10. Twenty five people attended the movie entitled Old Yeller

11. Yes you must read the magazine article entitled How to Be a Friend

12. Write your name in inverted form: _____

13. Fido my neighbors dog is cute

14. He has too many buts in his paragraph

15. One half of the class attended a pep assembly on Friday October 8 1993

39

A.   Sentence Types:
    Directions: Place correct punctuation at the end of each sentence
             and write the sentence type on the line.

1.   _____   Does he have a fever

2.   _____   Mark eats at his office desk

3.   _____   Stand at this line

4.   _____   I'm so excited

B.   Sentences, Fragments, and Run-Ons:
    Directions: Write **S** if the words form a sentence. Write **F** if the words
             form a fragment. Write **R-O** if the words form a run-on.

1.   ____   Watch out!

2.   ____   After they play tennis.

3.   ____   On the evening before departing on a cruise to the island of Aruba.

4.   ____   You seem cold, here take my extra blanket.

5.   ____   We have a new postal lady.

C.   Friendly Letters:
    Directions: Label the parts of this friendly letter:

                             2 Sea Way
         _____   **Otter Rock, OR   97388**
                             August 2, 20—

Dear Lani,   _____

      **Hi! I just want to give you our new address. We moved to Otter Rock
a few months ago. Oregon is so green from rain. It's a great place to hike, too!
Did you know that it is light until about nine here in the summer?** _____

                               Love, _____

                               Amy _____

D. Business Letters:
   Directions: Label the boldfaced part of this business letter **and** punctuate the salutation (greeting) correctly.

September 21, 20—

Success Concepts
Post Office Box 12   _____
Scottsdale, AZ   85155

Dear Mr. Phipps

E. Envelopes:
   Directions: Write your return address on this envelope. (You may create an address if you wish.)

_____

   _____

   _____

   _____

                                        _____

                                        _____

                                        _____

_____

F. Capitalization:
   Directions: Write a capital letter above any word that should be capitalized.

1. did general washington lead the continental army during the revolutionary war?

2. students from price middle school visited a spanish church in alamo square.

3. Last sunday, she entered davis memorial hospital for diabetes testing.

4. has dad learned about the roman empire in his college world history class?

5. can i take a ferry from ratton bay to ocracoke lighthouse in the south next fall?

6. mary pickford starred in an early movie entitled <u>tess of the storm country</u>.

G. Punctuation:
Directions: Insert needed punctuation.

1. Tate asked Wheres Peters black two piece suit

2. Judd meet me at 4 30 by the town hall the brick building on N Rue Way

3. On Friday May 20 2005 their son flew home and they all went out to celebrate

4. No we arent leaving for Sweet Grass Montana until our two sons game is over.

5. Ms Luna by the way has donated the following items beads sequins and wire

6. Yippee exclaimed Maria You won a prize a gift certificate for twenty dollars

H. Subjects and Verbs:
Directions: Underline the subject once and the verb or verb phrase twice.
Note: Crossing out prepositional phrases will help you.

1. Before bedtime, the young father likes to sit by his daughter's cradle.

2. Someone like Mark should apply for that job.

3. Joe and his son cannot lift this into the truck without your help.

4. Each of the students in that class must present a speech.

5. Follow the sidewalk by the well-lighted alley.

I. Contractions:
Directions: Write the contraction.

1. cannot - _____   3. you are - _____   5. will not - _____

2. what is - _____   4. they have - _____   6. they are - _____

J. Subject-Verb Agreement:
Directions: Underline the subject once. Underline the verb that agrees twice.

1. Their parents (belong, belongs) to a fishing club.

2. This splinter on my right thumb (hurt, hurts).

3. Only one of the new flight attendants (is, are) twenty-one.   43

K. Irregular Verbs:
  Directions: Underline the subject once and the correct verb phrase twice.

  1. Their windshield has been (broke, broken).

  2. By the end of the day, we will have (run, ran) two miles.

  3. Pets were (brung, brought) along.

  4. I must have (done, did) the wrong assignment.

  5. Have you (saw, seen) a yak?

  6. The seeds may have (sank, sunk) to the bottom of the pot.

  7. Wind must have (blown, blew) that tree down.

  8. I could not have (chose, chosen) a better gift.

  9. One of the swimmers has (swam, swum) in three races.

  10. The newspaper is (lying, laying) on a table.

  11. Sara might have (wrote, written) us a note.

  12. Jess had (drunk, drank) some orange juice.

  13. Some may have (went, gone) ahead.

  14. The children have (come, came) late for the performance.

  15. They should have (raised, risen) earlier.

L. Tenses:
  Directions: Underline the subject once and the verb or verb phrase
                      twice. Write the tense in the blank.

  1. _____ Will you join our team?

  2. _____ Leah peered through the telescope.

  3. _____ Cole weaves rugs.

M. Common and Proper Nouns:
    Directions: Place a ✓ if the noun is abstract.

1. ____ care   2. ____ carton   3. ____ patience

N. Singular and Plural Nouns:
    Directions: Write the correct spelling of each plural noun.

1. guess - _____   5. journey - _____

2. waltz - _____   6. paradox - _____

3. chairwoman - _____   7. courage - _____

4. penalty - _____   8. serf - _____

O. Possessive Nouns:
    Directions: Write the possessive in each blank.

1. an office building owned by more than one businessman -

    _____

2. a play area used by monkeys - _____

3. a trunk belonging to an elephant - _____

4. a vehicle belonging to Debi and Judi - _____

P. Identifying Nouns:
    Directions: Circle any nouns.

1. My idea is to take this shovel, a sleeping bag, two tents, and some strong rope.

Q. Usage and Knowledge:

1. Circle the correct answer: Do you know if (there, they're, their) in
                                  kindergarten?

2. Circle the correct answer: (Can, May) I come in?

3. Circle the correct answer: They completed the job (themselves, theirselves).

4. Write the antecedent of the possessive pronoun. Many eagles flew to their

   nests. _____

5. Place a dotted line under an interjection and a wavy line under a conjunction.

   Stand still or you may fall! Yikes!

6. Write a regular verb: _____

7. Circle the correct answer: You did that (perfect, perfectly).

8. Write a proper noun: _____

9. Circle the correct answer: I didn't buy (any, none).

10. Circle the correct answer: Our team played (good, well).

11. Write the antecedent of the possessive pronoun:

    You must give your full name. _____

12. Write a reflexive pronoun: _____

R. Identifying Adjectives:
   Directions: Circle any adjective.

1. An artist painted several bright blue flowers on two Chinese brass vases.

S. Degrees of Adjectives:
   Directions: Circle the correct answer.

1. This is the (more beautiful, most beautiful) ring of the entire collection.

2. This red helium balloon is (shinier, shiniest) of the five.

3. The taller of the two wrestlers is (more powerful, most powerful).

4. He is the (more respectful, most respectful) twin.

T. Adverbs:
   Directions: Circle any adverbs.

1. Jacy looks pale and doesn't feel very (good, well).

2. Stop acting so (weird, weirdly).

3. We don't want (none, any).

U. Identifying Adverbs:
   Directions: Circle any adverbs.

1. Two rather large dogs ran wildly together.

2. We will not arrive there tomorrow.

V. Degrees of Adverbs:
   Directions: Circle the correct answer.

1. Jack did his fourth exercise (more strenously, most strenuously).

2. Of the two contestants, Chessa throws the ball (harder, hardest).

3. That baby slept (more peacefully, most peacefully) on the third night.

4. I did (worse, worser, worst, worsest) on my second try.

W. Pronouns:
   Directions: Circle the correct answer.

1. Ringo, Hans, and (he, him) bought tickets for a ride.

2. (Me and my brother, My brother and me, My brother and I) are sweaty.

3. The ushers are Jana and (I, me).

4. I like (them, those) sparkling wands.

5. After the game, meet my brother and (I, me) outside.

6. Kim and (we, us) must finish putting away these tools.

7. (Who, Whom) did you ask?

8. Did the gardener and (they, them) seed the lawn?

9. The first ones chosen were Kate and (he, him).

10. My hair has lost (its, it's) luster.

11. Margo's brothers lost (his, their) place in line.

12. The boss handed Ben and (she, her) several packages.

13. (Who, Whom) is the artist of this modern painting?

14. Each of the women handed (her, their) keys to the valet.

15. One of the horses ran toward (its, their) colts.

X. Nouns and Pronouns Used as Subjects, Direct Objects, Indirect Objects, Objects of the Preposition, and Predicate Nominatives:

Directions: Look at the boldfaced word and decide how it is used in the sentence. Write **S.** for subject, **D.O.** for direct object, **I.O.** for indirect object, **O.P.** for object of the preposition, and **P.N.** for predicate nominative.

1. ____   Their **boss** quit yesterday.

2. ____   Terry is our **leader**.

3. ____   The dentist cleaned my **teeth**.

4. ____   She has gum in her **hair**.

5. ____   Mary and **I** play together.

Reflections

Preposition Test

_____

_____

_____

_____

_____

_____

_____

_____

_____

_____

_____

_____

Reflections

Verb Test

_____

_____

_____

_____

_____

_____

_____

_____

_____

_____

_____

_____

_____

Reflections

Noun Test

_____

_____

_____

_____

_____

_____

_____

_____

_____

_____

_____

Reflections

Adjective Test

_____

_____

_____

_____

_____

_____

_____

_____

_____

_____

_____

_____

_____

Reflections

Adverb Test

Reflections

Pronoun Test

_____

_____

_____

_____

_____

_____

_____

_____

_____

_____

_____

_____

_____

Reflections

Capitalization Test

_____

_____

_____

_____

_____

_____

_____

_____

_____

_____

_____

_____

_____

Reflections

Punctuation Test